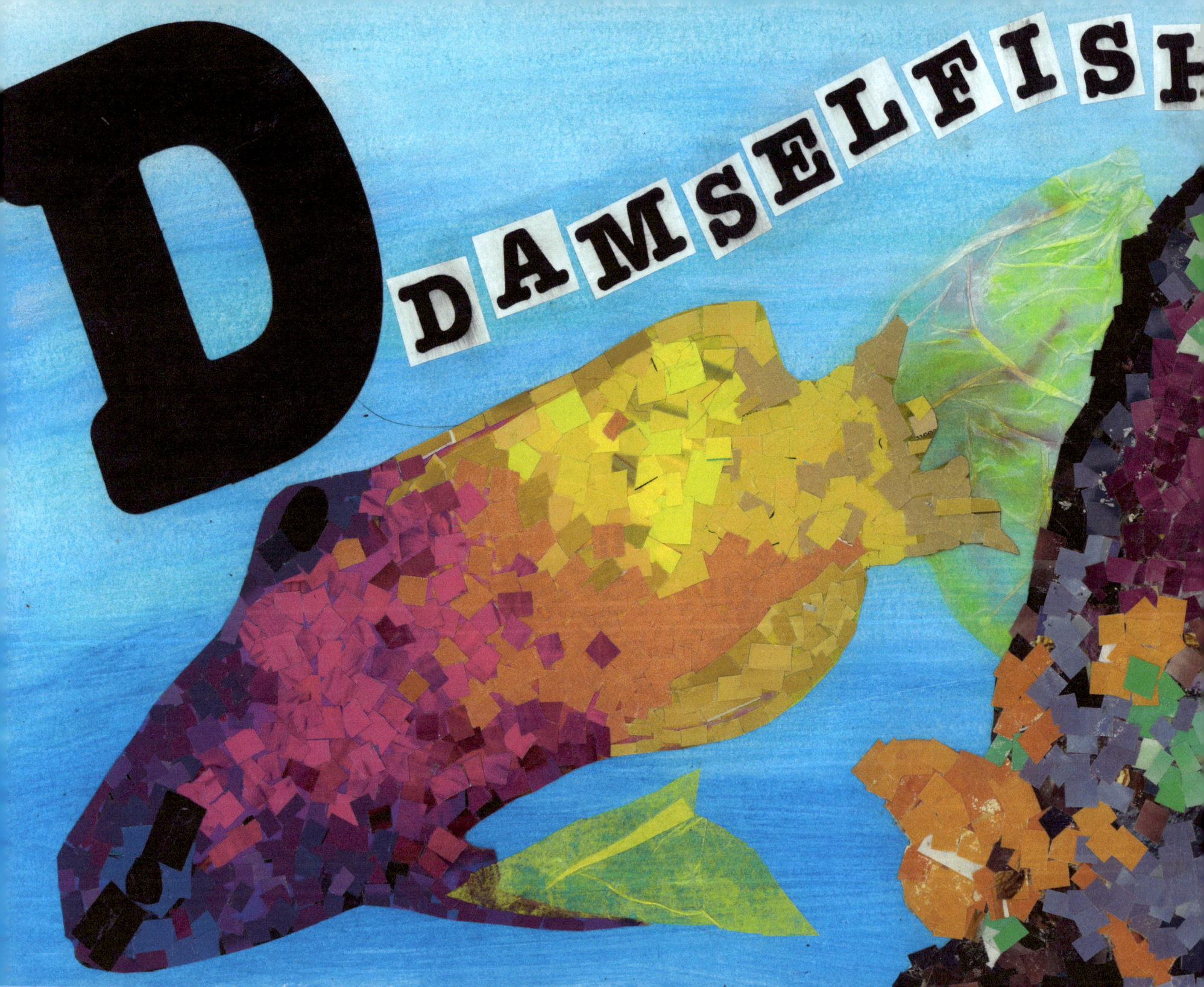

X Marks the Spot

Zebrafish

The vibrant existence of hundreds of species of sea life that live in the beautiful turquoise waters of the Caribbean Sea is what inspired Angi Shelangoski in creating her first children's book. The multimedia art used in these illustrations was created from recycled magazine pages and reclaimed tissue paper. It is Angi's hope to continue to create recycled multimedia works of art that will motivate children to read, dream and to create their own works of art.

Please visit Angi at Serendipity: The Art of Living and also note that 25% of the profit made from the sale of this book will be donated to Mary's Meals to help fund their schools in Haiti.

A Personal Note: My gratitude to the islands, waters, and life of the Caribbean Sea, Google, and snorkelstj.com for the inspiration of this book. Thank you also to all of my family and friends for your love and support!

www.ingramcontent.com/pod-product-compliance
Lightning Source LLC
Chambersburg PA
CBHW041326290426

44110CB00004B/155